‘I declare before you all that my whole life whether it be long or short shall be devoted to your service and the service of our great imperial family to which we all belong.’

Princess Elizabeth
21 April 1947

Contents

Photo: Anwar Hussein / Getty Images

The Princess Who Dazzled The World

'All the film people in the world, if they had scoured the globe, could not have found anyone so suited to the part.'

So said Winston Churchill, soon after Elizabeth's Coronation. Seven decades later it's hard to capture the sense of wonder, joy, and excitement that Elizabeth generated as she prepared to become Queen.

She sparkled.

Cecil Beaton, the great fashion photographer, said,

> *The unspoilt childishness of the smile, the pristine quality of her pink and white complexion, are all part of an appearance that is individual and gives the effect of a total entity.*

She was beautiful and also wholesome, vivacious and self-effacing, confident and humble. She embodied the possibility of a

Photo left: A portrait from the 1953 documentary film *A Queen is Crowned*

fresh start for nation and Commonwealth – spring after the long winter of war, austerity and rationing. Indeed, before 1953 was over, Churchill, who rarely spoke of God, wrote:

> *I regard it as the most direct mark of God's favour we have ever received in my long life that the whole structure of our new-formed Commonwealth has been linked and illuminated by a sparkling presence at its summit.*
>
> *The Faith of Queen Elizabeth*
> by Dudley Delffs

If he were alive today, I suspect Churchill would marvel even more at the grace of God to nation and Commonwealth. God, he believed, had chosen Elizabeth for this role. And Elizabeth, in awe and humility, saw it the same way.

Indeed, before Elizabeth Alexandra Mary Windsor began what was to become the longest reign in British history, there were two kings in her life.

There was the father she adored, King George VI, who, after his brother's

Photo above: Prince Charles and Princess Anne waiting while their mother chats to Winston Churchill abdication, had wholeheartedly embraced the responsibilities of the crown that he had never expected to wear.

And there was her God to whom she was entirely devoted.

At her Coronation in Westminster Abbey, Elizabeth made several promises before her God and her people:

She promised to serve him and his church.

She promised to serve the people of the United Kingdom and the peoples of the Commonwealth.

She promised to rule with justice and mercy.

She made those promises with words written by other people, but six months before, it was in her own words that she asked the people of the United Kingdom and Commonwealth to:

> *Pray that God may give me wisdom and strength to carry out the solemn promises I shall be making, and that I may faithfully serve him and you, all the days of my life.*

After over 70 years in the role, no one would dispute that she kept those promises. But she did it in such a kind and determined, dignified and down-to-earth, wise and wholesome way that she won not only the gratitude and affection of her richly diverse nation, but also the respect and admiration of hundreds of millions of people around the world.

Still, it is one thing to appreciate and honour someone's achievements, it's another to understand what has enabled them to excel. What, then, was the secret of a life so well lived in the public eye?

Curiously, although we know very little about what the Queen thought about a whole host of issues, she was crystal clear about the source of her strength, pointing with characteristic humility away from herself:

> *I know just how much I rely on my faith to guide me though the good times and the bad. Each day is a new beginning. I know that the only way to live my life is to try to do what is right, to take the long view, to give of my best in all that the day brings, and to put my trust in God. I draw strength from the message of hope in the Christian gospel.*

Christmas 2002

Her answer goes some way to explaining how she could be so extraordinary and yet so down-to-earth, so celebrated and yet so modest, so uniquely privileged and yet so attuned to the needs of others.

Many biographers have noted the significance of her Christian faith; this tribute seeks to explore it. Faith in God is often seen as a support in hard times, a source of comfort, strength and wisdom in the trials of life. For Elizabeth that was only part of it. Her faith was just as vital in the good times as the tough times. It shaped how she saw her successes; her times of high popularity, good health, diplomatic successes, family growth, wins at Ascot...

> *For me the teachings of Christ and my own personal accountability before God provide a framework in which I try to lead my life.*
>
> Christmas 2000

At the heart of this was her understanding of her call to a life of service modelled on Jesus:

> *This is the time of the year when we remember that God sent his only Son 'to serve, not to be served'. He restored love and service to the centre of our lives in the person of Jesus Christ...*
>
> Christmas 2012

It was her trust in his ways that taught her to 'give of my best in all that the day brings,' from advising Prime Minister after Prime Minister to tramping across heather-clad hills, from agreeing seating plans for state banquets to laying and clearing the table at her log cabin barbecues on the Balmoral Estate.

In Elizabeth's life, faith was like yeast in bread. Yeast is not the only ingredient in bread but it's the one that makes all the difference. Indeed, trying to understand the Queen without understanding her relationship with God is like trying to understand an apple without looking at the tree.

And, even as a young girl, the tree was already budding.

Photo right: Queen Elizabeth II arriving back in England from Kenya after the death of her father, 1952

The Child Who Knew The Way

'Go out into the darkness and put your hand into the Hand of God. That shall be to you better than light...'

It was December 1939. Elizabeth was 13. Back in July, she had met and been mesmerised by the man that she would one day marry.

The war was three months old and her father, King George VI, was struggling over what he might say in his Christmas address to a nation that had, only 20 years before, fought a war against Germany that had cost millions of lives. No one was under any illusion that this conflict would be less costly in blood or destruction. What do you say to a people who are about to undergo terrible loss and suffering?

Elizabeth offered her father a poem by Minnie Louise Haskins to consider. In his broadcast, King George quoted these lines:

Photo left: Princess Elizabeth confidently greeting the Officer of the Guard when arriving for a rehearsal of the Aldershot Tattoo, 1935

And I said to the man who stood at the gate of the year:

'Give me a light that I may tread safely into the unknown.'

And he replied:

'Go out into the darkness and put your hand into the Hand of God.

That shall be to you better than light and safer than a known way.'

It is not a poem that promises escape or ease or even victory. It is a poem that promises God's companionship, presence, wisdom, guidance. It is a poem about a God who is there and holds out his hand. And can be trusted, come what may. It is an invitation to walk with him.

It would not be the last time Elizabeth would offer that poem to others.

It was this poem that she quoted in the only foreword she contributed to a book. The book was *The Servant Queen and the King She Serves*, a book that focused on the dynamism of her

Photo above: Learning from her father - Princess Elizabeth with King George VI in a Buckingham Palace office
Photo right: Mourning alone at Prince Philip's funeral

Christian faith, published to celebrate her 90th birthday. And it was this poem too that she offered as her contribution to a collection of reflections published in 2018.

On 9 April 2021, Philip, the man who captivated Elizabeth some 82 years before, lay in his bed in Windsor Castle, his family around him, and breathed his last. Describing the moment, Sophie, Countess of Wessex said,

> *It was so gentle. It was like someone took him by the hand, and then he went.*

This is the God Elizabeth gave her hand to, not just at the gate of every year, but at the gate of every day of her long reign. The God who is always ready to receive any hand stretched out to him in trust.

And the God who comes to take our hands when we no longer have the strength to offer them.

The Woman Who Was Chosen From Above

In simple attire, dressed as an ordinary woman, she readied herself to be anointed. God had called her. And he would equip her.

It was the most watched event in television history up to that time.

Some 27 million tuned in and a further 11 million listened on the radio. Elizabeth had, at first, been reluctant to have any of the Westminster Abbey service televised, but Philip, ahead of his time as he would often be, saw the opportunity to bring the country together, to help her connect to a nation still under rationing but yearning for a brighter, better future. She agreed. But there was one moment where Elizabeth insisted that the cameras should turn away. The moment of her anointing with oil.

Her regalia had just been removed – the crimson velvet robe, the diamond diadem

Photo left: A Coronation day portrait, 2 June 1953

and the Coronation necklace. All that was left was a woman in a simple white dress. She looked like a bride – young, delicate, beautiful – except that the dress was so much simpler than the one she wore at her wedding. The contrast would have been startling to anyone who'd seen the pictures of that wedding dress – and who hadn't – with its 15-foot satin train.

And it was in this simple attire, dressed as an ordinary woman, that she readied herself to be anointed.

And then she disappeared from public view.

A private moment in this most public of occasions. A private moment that set the terms of the public office.

God had called her.

And so the Archbishop poured anointing oil onto her hands, her chest and her head to indicate that she had been set apart to love and serve God and her people with all her strength, with all her heart, and with all her mind. That is, as Queen, she was to fulfil what Jesus called the greatest commandment:

> *Love the Lord your God with all your heart and with all your soul and with all your strength and with all your mind' and, 'Love your neighbour as yourself.*

The Bible: Luke's Gospel 10:27

Later, her mother would say that this anointing, not the actual setting of St Edward's Crown on her

Photo above: Princess Elizabeth on her wedding day, 1947

head, was the most significant moment in Elizabeth's life. It carried for her what biographer William Shawcross called an almost 'sacrificial quality'. Like Christ, whose name means 'anointed one', she was anointed not to be served by her people but to give her life in service to her people for her God.

That was the commitment she made.
And she embraced it wholeheartedly.

We shouldn't take that for granted. After all, Elizabeth's uncle, King Edward VIII, had abdicated after less than a year. Furthermore, the life of a minor royal might well have suited Elizabeth admirably: away from the limelight and the lenses, looking after a country estate, bringing up her children, being heavily involved in the training and racing of horses. But that was not Elizabeth's path. And she saw God's hand in it. It was he who had chosen her for this role. And the anointing was the moment when God confirmed his choice and empowered her for the challenges ahead.

She had made promises to him. And he in turn had promised to help her in what he had called her to do, as he promises us all. He kept his promise to her. As she put it in 1981:

> *Christ not only revealed to us the truth in his teachings. He lived by what he believed and gave us the strength to try to do the same...*

This, she believed, was how she was able to keep her promises to God, and to us.

Photo above: Queen Elizabeth II dressed simply in white for her anointing in Westminster Abbey, 1953

"I want to thank everyone on the NHS frontline as well as care workers and those carrying out essential roles"
Her Majesty The Queen
Message to the Nation
Photo: PA Media
BARCLAYS
Boots
GAP
WICKED

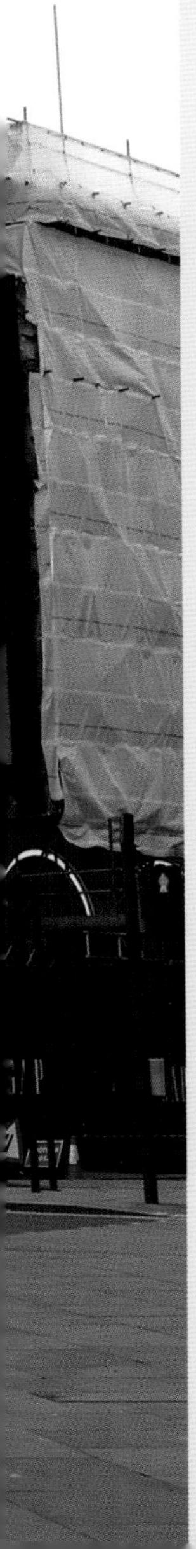

The Patriot Who Called Us To Our Best

'The pride in who we are is not a part of our past, it defines our present and our future.'

Over the decades of her record-breaking reign the Queen travelled more than a million miles to more than 100 countries. And whilst we may see more pictures of her on ceremonial occasions and at glittering events, the reality is that she spent far more of her time visiting hospitals, care homes, schools, factories, enterprises and the over 600 charities of which she was patron.

> *My work, and the work of my family, takes us every week into that quiet sort of public life, where millions of people give their time, unpaid and usually unsung, to the community.*
>
> Christmas 1998

She was a champion of the volunteer spirit.

Photo left: A grateful message from the Queen displayed in London's Piccadilly Circus during the Covid pandemic

And whilst she never had the political power to directly affect government policy, that did not mean that she didn't have a vision for the kind of country she hoped we would become:

> *I cannot lead you into battle, I do not give you laws or administer justice but I can do something else. I can give you my heart and my devotion to these old islands and to all the people of our brotherhood of nations. I believe in our qualities and in our strength. I believe that together we can set an example to the world which will encourage upright people everywhere...*

Christmas 1957

In the context of Britain's imperial past this is a remarkable vision. It is not a vision of military superiority, economic dominance, creative brilliance, or sporting excellence but of moral example. A vision that would not inspire envy or fear but encourage generosity, justice, kindness, 'uprightness'. It is similar to God's original hope for the people of Israel in the Bible, that they would be 'a light to the nations'.

Over the years in her broadcasts she highlighted the particular qualities she valued – resilience, kindness, neighbourliness – qualities she'd seen in the wartime generation. When she spoke to the nation during the Covid pandemic she once again focused on those qualities, summoning us to live up to our heritage:

> *I hope in the years to come, everyone will be able to take pride in how they responded to this challenge. And those who come after us will say the Britons of this generation were as strong as any. That the attributes of self-discipline, quiet, good-humoured resolve and of fellow-feeling still characterise this country. The pride in who we are is not a part of our past, it defines our present and our future.*
>
> 5 April 2020

Now, you can tell a lot about a person by what they choose to praise. When the England team won the European Women's Football Championships,

Photo left: Laughter puts people at ease – the Queen at Windsor presenting the George Cross to representatives of the National Health Service, July 2022
Photo above: Captain Sir Thomas Moore receiving the insignia of Knight Bachelor at Windsor Castle, July 2020

the Queen affirmed their excellent performance and importantly chose to congratulate the support staff as well as the entire team.

> *Your success goes far beyond the trophy you have so deservedly earned.*
>
> *You have all set an example that will be an inspiration for girls and women today, and for future generations.*
>
> *It is my hope that you will be as proud of the impact you have had on your sport as you are of the result today.*

The Queen affirmed the success the team had 'earned' which is about the effort put in. And she affirmed the 'impact' their efforts would have on their sport. Furthermore, she reminded them that they had become a role model to others. Again, something the Queen was always acutely aware of. With status and success come responsibility to others.

Intrinsic to her understanding of her own, and our, responsibility was her understanding of what it means to be a good neighbour. Time and again, in her Christmas addresses, she encouraged us to reach out to the marginalised, the excluded, the struggling, the lonely, the grieving, the hungry. Several times she referred to the parable of the Good Samaritan, a story Jesus told in response to the question: who is my neighbour? Here's what she said in 2020 in the middle of the Covid crisis:

> *We continue to be inspired by the kindness of strangers and draw comfort that – even on the darkest nights – there is hope in the new dawn.*
>
> *Jesus touched on this with the parable of the Good Samaritan. The man who is robbed and left at the roadside is saved by someone who did not share his religion or culture. This wonderful story of kindness is still as relevant today. Good Samaritans have emerged across society showing care and respect for all, regardless of gender, race or background, reminding us that each one of us is special and equal in the eyes of God. The teachings of Christ have served as my inner light...*

Yes, the Queen was a firm believer in Christ, and sought to imitate him, but she was aware, as he was, that kindness

is not the preserve of particular creeds or races. Indeed, in Jesus' time the Samaritans were despised by the Jews, dismissed as religiously misguided and racially impure, shunned as unclean – the last people you'd expect to do a kind deed for a stranger.

The Queen brought out a point that is rarely made: the Samaritan is not just being kind when others weren't, he is being kind to someone who is most likely of a different race and religion from himself. In the year when the Black Lives Matter campaign exploded into life around the world, the Queen, without drawing attention to the issues, reminded the many peoples of the Commonwealth and multi-ethnic, multi-faith Britain of our responsibility to one another.

Indeed, she always sought to give her best and to call us all to ours. You can see this again and again in the way she engaged with people in everyday situations. Stories abound.

Here's one.

Photo above: The Queen, delighted to receive a gift during a visit to a Scunthorpe mosque on her Golden Jubilee tour

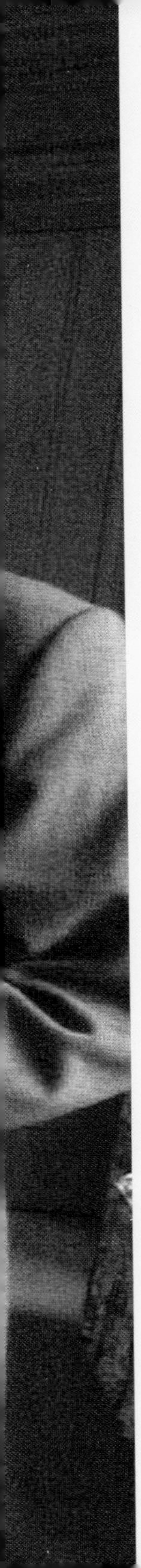

The Lady Who Brought The Lamps

'Christ's example helps me see the value of doing small things with great love.' Queen Elizabeth II

Scotland, August 2005. It's warm and sunny and the midges are out in clouds. The green Land Rover pulls up in front of the cottage that sits snugly on the low hill. The driver steps out, a woman in walking shoes and a sensible tweed skirt. She goes to the back of the car, pulls out two table lamps, and walks towards the cottage.

Inside, five teenagers and two adults are waiting – an ordinary family in a rented holiday cottage. They're excited, a bit nervous, and considerably neater than they normally would be on a holiday in the Scottish countryside. The cottage is neater too. Even the boot room was tidied.

Photo left: The Queen and Prince Philip on holiday at Balmoral Castle in Scotland, 2005

Meanwhile, making her way towards the front door carrying two table lamps is a 79-year-old woman, the most famous woman in the world, the most photographed woman in the world, one of the richest women in the world, the woman who at that point had already advised 12 Prime Ministers, and met with the heads of state of over 110 countries; the woman who had 491 full-time staff working for her across four residences, and who owned the 50,000 acre estate they were staying on. This was the cottage she holidayed in with her parents and sister when she was growing up – when it was just 'Us Four', as they called themselves. She'd had a hankering to look around. And had asked if they minded if she popped in.

And so in she pops, relaxes everyone instantly, chats a bit, and does a joyous impression of a hunched backpacker trudging across the Balmoral Estate. Then she looks around and puts the lamps in the master bedroom – she'd heard that the light wasn't too good for reading in the evening, and so here she is sorting it herself, rather than delegating it to one of the 100 or so staff on the estate. As it turned out she was particularly interested in the boot room: it was where she and her sister had played ping-pong. Thank goodness they'd tidied it.

And when she left, they thought, 'Wasn't that lovely? Wasn't she so relaxed, so down-to-earth, so authentic?' And they felt privileged, blessed. Actually, 'honoured' was the word used. Honoured.

A few years later some of the same family were visiting the Sandringham Estate. And they picked up the same feeling.

The staff – the stable hands, the cooks, the managers – all knew that the Queen loved the place, knew what was going on, and cared about them. They'd seen it themselves, or heard it from a hundred little stories. She gave them more than respect. Respect is too cold a word. After all, you can respect an ogre. No, she appreciated what they did. Honoured them. There was a kind of joy in the air. The door handle shone not just because the cleaner wanted to do a really good job but because the Queen would be using it, and the cleaner wanted to honour the Queen, because the Queen, they sensed, honoured them.

Here's what she said in 2016 about the value of small things:

> *Jesus Christ lived obscurely for most of his life, and never travelled far. He was maligned and rejected by many, though he had done no wrong. And yet, billions of people now follow his teaching and find in him the guiding light for their lives. I am one of them because Christ's example helps me see the value of doing small things with great love, whoever does them and whatever they themselves believe.*
>
> *The message of Christmas reminds us that inspiration is a gift to be given as well as received, and that love begins small but always grows.*

Yes, at New Year, and to mark her birthday, the Queen conferred honours on people who had contributed in particularly impactful ways to nation and Commonwealth. But for her, there seemed to be two other honours lists.

Photo above: The Queen's family, including her grandson Peter, and the royal corgis at Balmoral, 1979 (Ron Bell / Camera Press)

There were the people Her Majesty worked with and met along the way, and honoured in the way she engaged with them; and there were also the people who made a significant contribution, not so much because of their particular role, but because of the way they lived their lives – the everyday honours list. So, in her 1980 Christmas message, she thanked all those who contributed to the flourishing of the nation – from medics to educators, from the Armed Forces to people working in commerce, and she concluded in this way:

> *And I include all those who don't realise that they deserve thanks and are content that what they do is unseen and unrewarded. The very act of living a decent and upright life is in itself a positive factor in maintaining civilised standards.*

Everyone matters.

And where does that deep, deep understanding come from? This story gives us a clue, I think.

December 2010. St Mary Magdalene's, Sandringham. The congregation is gathering. A five-foot-four woman slips in the side door and takes a seat, as she does in some church every Sunday, almost without fail. She stands up when everyone else stands up, she sits when everyone else sits, she sings when everyone else sings, bows her head in prayer when everyone else bows, and listens to the sermon as everyone else does.

The Supreme Governor of the Church of England goes to gather with God's people, to praise him, to pray to him, to confess her sins, to ask for forgiveness, and to seek wisdom and strength for the coming week. As she put it:

> *The teachings of Christ have served as my inner light, as has the sense of purpose we can find in coming together to worship.*

Notice the 'we' in that sentence: God's wisdom and peace is available to all. We are all equal before God, equal before the God in whose image, she believes, every person on the face of the planet has been created.

How could she in turn not honour every person?

Photo left: Essays on what they would do as queen for a day won these girls in Pretoria, South Africa, an audience with Her Majesty, 1999

1932
1938
1939
1942
1956
1961
1965
1967
1986
1988
1989
1992
2005
2007
2012
2016

1947
1948
1952
1953
1971
1975
1977
1981
1993
1997
2000
2002
2017
2019
2020
2022

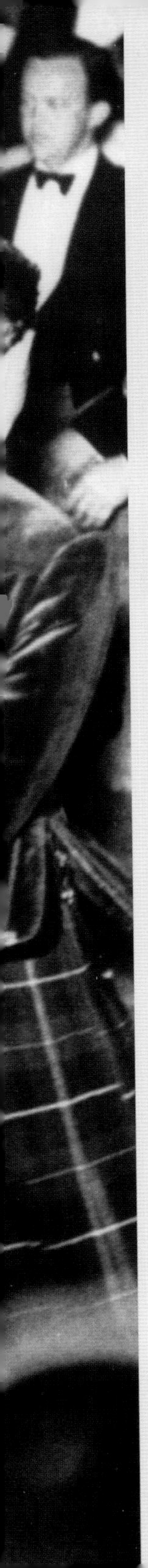

The Dancer Who Wooed The Nations

'The Commonwealth is… built on the highest qualities of the spirit of man: friendship, loyalty, and the desire for freedom and peace.' Queen Elizabeth II

Elizabeth had a clear desire for Britain to be an influence for good in the world, not through imperial power but in moral stature. She was one of the great internationalists. Few things demonstrate that commitment more clearly than all she did to build, nurture and strengthen the Commonwealth.

When Elizabeth was born, the British Empire embraced a quarter of the earth's surface and it's monarch reigned over nearly 460 million people. By 1953, it had shrunk dramatically, as nation after nation gained independence. It was a process that would continue. It was replaced by the Commonwealth, initially an association of just eight nations, primarily ruled by people of white descent. Today, the Commonwealth includes 56 independent and equal countries across four continents.

Photo left: Princess Elizabeth dancing at the Royal Caledonian Tartan Ball, 1946

How do you turn nations you have conquered, ruled and exploited for decades into friends?

How has it happened that, in our deeply fractured world, 56 nations should choose to meet regularly, not out of military expediency or shared religion or vital economic self-interest but out of a commitment to a common vision for a different kind of world?

The short answer is through the determination, warmth, and relational skills of the Queen. When she took the throne she said,

> *The Commonwealth bears no resemblance to the empires of the past. It is an entirely new conception built on the highest qualities of the spirit of man: friendship, loyalty, and the desire for freedom and peace. To that new conception of an equal partnership of nations and races I shall give myself heart and soul every day of my life.*

It was another promise she would keep. At the Silver Jubilee, she said that she had witnessed:

> *From a unique position ... the last great phase of the Empire into Commonwealth and the transformation of the Crown from a n emblem of dominion into a symbol of free and voluntary association. In all history, this has no precedent.*

Photo above: Young leaders from across the Commonwealth with the Queen, former Prime Minister Sir John Major and footballer David Beckham at Buckingham Palace, 2015

Interestingly, this was a vision that she was more committed to than any of her governments or most of the British people. But it demonstrated once again her fundamental commitment to human equality. Indeed, as the rows about removing statues of imperial figures and slave owners and repenting of our imperial past rolled on across Britain, even to the point in 2021 of one Oxford college removing a portrait of the Queen, she herself had transformed the relationship with the nations we had oppressed.

This commitment to equality had its roots in her understanding of Jesus. As she put it in 1982,

> *Christ attached supreme importance to the individual and he amazed the world in which he lived by making it clear that the unfortunate and the underprivileged had an equal place in the Kingdom of Heaven with the rich and powerful.*

So it was with nations. The Commonwealth was no G7, ranking nations by GDP. Each nation met as an equal. So, in her Christmas address after the 2012 London Olympics, she rejoiced in Commonwealth successes:

> *Grenada, the Bahamas, Jamaica and New Zealand won more medals per head of population than any other countries.*

Where did the Queen get such a vision?

It was an idea that belonged to neither the left nor the right. In reality, it comes straight out of the biblical promise of a day when the tanks will be turned into tractors, or to quote the Bible, 'spears into ploughshares': a day when nation will not fight against nation, when peace will reign across the globe. Elizabeth knew that it would only be fully realised when Christ returned but that did not stop her working to create a context in which understanding could grow, cooperation flourish, and inequalities be addressed.

Still, it is one thing to have a vision, it is quite another to turn it into a living reality. How did she do it?

By making friends.

In 1961, the Queen went on an 11-day tour of Ghana, a former colony enjoying its independence under Africa's most influential Black leader Kwame Nkrumah. Nkrumah had been imprisoned by the British but, by 1957, he had secured the country's independence. Still, Western powers were concerned that Nkrumah, now President, would be lured into the Soviet sphere. The Queen's tour was seen as an opportunity to help prevent that. But as it came to the final farewell ball it was not clear which way Nkrumah would sway.

And so, on that evening the Queen asked Nkrumah to dance – a risk of sorts; what if he'd said 'no' or scowled at her throughout? But this was not first a political move but a relational one, as if she were saying, 'It's a ball. Let's dance. Let's be friends and see where that takes us.'

The joy of the dance is there in the photographs and whilst it did not have the kind of short-term impact on Nkrumah's foreign policy attributed to it by Netflix's *The Crown,* it did communicate a powerful message about the Queen as a person. At a time when racism was rife in Britain, when Black people couldn't eat in the same restaurant as white people in the southern United States, and when apartheid oppressed the majority Black population in South Africa, here was a sparkling white Queen dancing with the charismatic Black leader of a former colony.

And dancing rather well, as it happens.

More broadly, it was precisely the Queen's relational approach that created the friendly, almost familial culture of the Commonwealth. She called it her 'favourite club'. This warmth not only influenced the formal meetings but the atmosphere at the four-yearly Commonwealth Games. No surprise then that they're dubbed 'The Friendly Games'. Athletes don't just come to compete, they come to meet one another and celebrate each other's nations.

Refreshing, isn't it?

Photo above: The dancing Queen with Ghana's president Kwame Nkrumah, 1961

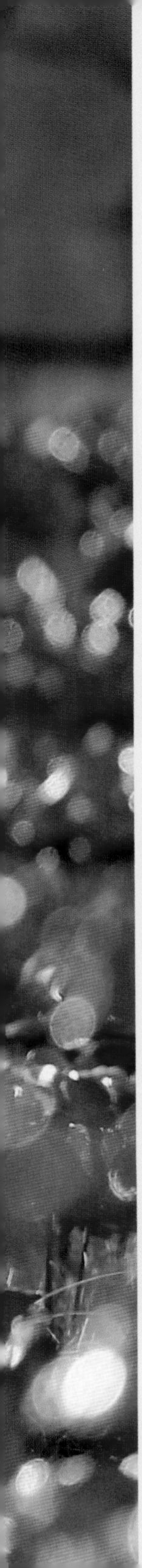

The Rider Who Rode The Storms

'As dark as death can be . . . light and life are greater. May the living flame of the Easter hope be a steady guide . . .' Queen Elizabeth II

It was 11 April 2021, and the world was still in the grip of the Covid pandemic. Over 127,000 had already died in Britain alone. For the first time in her reign the Queen chose to send out an audio Easter message. After recognising the importance of light as a symbol of hope in many religions, she said:

> *The discovery of the risen Christ on the first Easter Day gave his followers new hope and fresh purpose, and we can all take heart from this. We know that Coronavirus will not overcome us. As dark as death can be – particularly for those suffering with grief – light and life are greater. May the living flame of the Easter hope be a steady guide as we face the future.*

It is message of hope beyond this life, and of purpose in this life, despite its trials and griefs.

Photo left: Remembering the fallen in a field of ceramic poppies at the Tower of London, October 2014

A year later, the world watched her, dressed in black, sitting alone in a pew in the chapel of St George at Windsor. Twenty-nine other members of the family were scattered in a chapel big enough for 800. In front of her was the coffin of the man she had known for over 82 years. On the coffin, by the floral bouquet, sat a small white card, signed Lilibet. It was the nickname she got as a child because she couldn't say 'Elizabeth' and Lilibet was as close as she could get. A wife's farewell, not a monarch's.

How would the Queen respond to his loss? Perhaps it was precisely her deep belief in life after death that enabled her to return to public life so swiftly and with such evident joy, despite her husband's death, despite the painful accusations that had been levelled at the Royal Household by the Duke and Duchess of Sussex, and despite the pandemic.

Indeed, just two months later, when she arrived for the last day of Royal Ascot, she seemed to beam with happiness

to be there once again. Similarly, when she joined the June meeting of the G7, and the leaders were getting ready for the socially distanced photograph, she quipped, 'Are you supposed to be looking as if you're enjoying yourselves?' And, of course, after that, everyone did.

Death loses some of its sting when you know that it is the doorway into new life.

Of course, Elizabeth had been through many a storm. She grew up during a world war that killed 75 million people. Her father died young. She lost her mother and her younger sister in the same year and she outlived all her childhood friends. Her first home as a married woman burned down, and then in 1992 Windsor Castle suffered terrible fire damage. In the same year, Prince Andrew separated from his wife, Princess Anne divorced her husband, the book *Diana: Her True Story*, about the Princess of Wales, was published revealing the unhappiness of her marriage to Charles. It was much covered in the media, as indeed was Charles' affair with Camilla.

Photo left: Inspecting the damage after the Windsor Castle fire, 1992
Photo above: On the 40th anniversary of her reign, in a speech at London's Guildhall, the Queen described 1992 as an 'Annus Horribilis' (Anwar Hussein / Getty Images)

That November, the Queen gave a speech at the Guildhall in the City of London:

> *1992 is not a year on which I shall look back with undiluted pleasure. In the words of one of my more sympathetic correspondents, it has turned out to be an 'Annus Horribilis'. I suspect that I am not alone in thinking it so. Indeed, I suspect that there are very few people or institutions unaffected by these last months of worldwide turmoil and uncertainty.*

Typically, despite her own trials, she turned the spotlight away from herself. Then she went on to reveal another source of her strength:

> *You, my Lord Mayor, and all those whose prayers – fervent, I hope, but not too frequent – have sustained me through all these years, are friends indeed. Prince Philip and I give you all, wherever you may be, our most humble thanks.*

In a secular age, it is unusual to hear a leading international figure, unless they are a religious leader, talk about

Photo above: After attending a private service at Crathie Church, the royal family stopped to look at floral tributes left for Princess Diana at the gates of Balmoral, September 1997

prayer in a major public speech. The Queen didn't have to. She chose to. Perhaps simply because when times are tough, the knowledge that other people are praying to God on your behalf is wonderfully heartening.

In 2013, she put it this way:

> *For Christians, as for all people of faith, reflection, meditation and prayer help us to renew ourselves in God's love, as we strive daily to become better people. The Christmas message shows us that this love is for everyone. There is no one beyond its reach.*

Prayer – talking and listening to God – brings perspective and strength. Prayer leads to a renewed sense of God's love and care, to a renewed sense of security and worth. For her it was a daily practice.

And just as the Queen appreciated other people's prayers for her, so she prayed for others, and for us:

> *It is my prayer that on this Christmas Day we might all find room in our lives for the message of the angels and for the love of God through Christ our Lord.*

Christmas 2011

Photo above: Queen Elizabeth the Queen Mother at the Royal Lodge, Windsor, celebrating her 80th birthday with her two daughters, 1980

This sense that Christ shaped how she responded to adversity and helped her through it was a frequent theme:

> *I hope that, like me, you will be comforted by the example of Jesus of Nazareth who, often in circumstances of great adversity, managed to live an outgoing, unselfish and sacrificial life... He makes it clear that genuine human happiness and satisfaction lie more in giving than receiving; more in serving than in being served. We can surely be grateful that, two thousand years after the birth of Jesus, so many of us are able to draw inspiration from his life and message, and to find in him a source of strength and courage.*
>
> Christmas 2008

More broadly, the Queen had a calm about her.

Nothing seemed to phase her. In 1981, at the Trooping of the Colour, six shots were fired at her from the crowd – blanks as it turned out, but no one knew that until later. Her horse, Burmese, was startled, but the Queen, riding side-saddle, calmed him, and rode on. In 1982, a middle-aged male intruder appeared in her bedroom at Buckingham Palace at about 6.45am. She didn't panic, scream, or try to run away. Later, asked why she was so calm, she replied:

> *You seem to forget that I spend most of my time conversing with complete strangers.*

'Yes, Ma'am,' someone might have replied, 'but not people who have evaded all your security officers, and turned up uninvited and unannounced in your bedroom before dawn.'

This sense of ease was something that people picked up on quickly. One of her many portraitists, Chris Levine, spent less than an hour with her in 2004 and entitled his holographic portraits *Lightness of Being* and *Equanimity*.

So, it was to Jesus she turned in prayer to sustain her. It was to his example she looked in the many challenges she faced and it was to his teaching she turned to shape her priorities, her decisions and her responses to her critics.

Photo right: The Queen's horse bolted after shots were fired during the Trooping the Colour, June 1981

The Woman Who Forgave The Bombers

'For me, the life of Jesus Christ . . . is an inspiration and an anchor in my life. A role-model of reconciliation and forgiveness . . .' Queen Elizabeth II

Over the decades the Queen was accused of a whole host of things: of being a poor mother, a bad sister, of being dull, out of touch, grumpy, indifferent to the pain of her people, of running a racist household, of being a drain on the public purse, of being a symbol of our oppressive, imperialistic, colonial past, of making no significant contribution to our national life.

How do people in the public eye tend to respond to criticism and accusations?

Well, first, they do actually tend to respond. And, secondly, they often respond with a barrage of impassioned denials, scalding outrage, counter-accusatory tweets and incendiary Instagram posts.

Photo left: Shaking hands with Northern Ireland Deputy First Minister Martin McGuinness in Belfast, Northern Ireland, 2012

The Queen never responded to her critics with counter-accusations or outraged denials. Often, she did not respond at all. And when she did it was usually with very few, very well-chosen words.

When Meghan, Prince Harry's wife, expressed her hurt and disappointment at the way she felt she had been treated by the Royal Household, one of the Palace's press releases included the phrase, 'Recollections may vary.' It was a way of recognising someone else's perspective without agreeing with it, or attributing any malicious motives to them, or denying that they might be right. The Queen didn't stoke the fire, she damped it down. The Sussexes would 'always be much loved family members'. It was a way of keeping the door open to reconciliation and forgiveness.

This theme of forgiveness was one that the Queen returned to again and again in her Christmas addresses. In 1984, she said:

> *Above all, we must retain the child's readiness to forgive, with which we are all born and which it is all too easy to lose as we grow older. Without it, divisions between families, communities and nations remain unbridgeable. We owe it to our children and grandchildren to live up to the standards of behaviour and tolerance which we are so eager to teach them.*
>
> *It is particularly at Christmas, which marks the birth of the Prince of Peace, that we should work to heal old wounds and to abandon prejudice and suspicion. What better way of making a start than by remembering what Christ said – 'Except ye become as little children, ye shall not enter into the Kingdom of Heaven'.*

In 1976, 297 people had died as a result of bombings or shootings in the decades-long conflict in Northern Ireland. In her Christmas address, the Queen said, without mentioning any particular place:

> *The gift I would value next year is that reconciliation should be found wherever it is needed. A reconciliation which would bring peace and security to families and neighbours at present suffering and torn apart.*

Three years later it was a gift that she and her family particularly needed after the assassination of Earl Mountbatten by the Provisional IRA. But the Queen and her family always fought hard for peace and reconciliation among her people and between communities. So it was that in 2011 she made a successful state visit to the Republic of Ireland. So it was that she shook the hand of a representative of the Provisional IRA who had been involved in violent action. So it was that in 2012 she met with representatives of both sides of the conflict in Northern Ireland. So it was that she became the first British monarch to meet the Pope since Henry VIII decided to cede from Rome in 1533. So it was that in 2002, just months after the Al Qaeda attacks on the USA on 9/11, she chose to visit a mosque in Scunthorpe. Afzal Khan, Secretary there, said:

> *There was a lot of anxiety (at that time) among the Muslim community. On both sides actually. And it was a great gesture from Her*

Photo above: Members of the royal family on the balcony of Buckingham Palace watching the Trooping the Colour flypast, 2018

Majesty to come to the mosque at that time to show that it doesn't matter what happened, nobody can divide us. We are one nation and one people.

Jawaid Ishaq, Chairman of South Humber Racial Equality Council, summed it up:

She is Queen for all of us.

She was. Yes, she was a woman of strong Christian conviction, but that didn't lead her to dismiss people of other faiths or none. On the contrary, it led her to reach out, to give them the same respect and dignity she gave to those who shared her beliefs. Former Chief Rabbi Jonathan Sacks recalls this moving occasion:

Punctuality, said Louis XVIII of France, is the politeness of kings. Royalty arrives on time and leaves on time. So it is with Her Majesty the Queen, with one memorable exception.

The day was 27 January 2005, the sixtieth anniversary of the liberation of Auschwitz, and the place, St James's Palace. The Queen was meeting a group of Holocaust survivors. When the time came for her to leave, she stayed. And stayed. One of her attendants said he had never known her to linger so long after her scheduled departure time. She gave each survivor – it was a large group – her focused, unhurried attention. She stood with each until they had finished telling their personal story.

It was an act of kindness that almost had me in tears. One after another, the survivors were coming to me in a kind of trance, saying, 'Sixty years ago I did not know whether I would be alive tomorrow, and here I am today talking to the Queen.' It brought a kind of blessed closure into deeply lacerated lives.

We do not always appreciate the role the Queen has played in the transformation of Britain into a multi-ethnic, multi-faith society. No one does interfaith better than the Royal family, and it starts with the Queen herself.

This commitment to understanding and mutual respect is not an accident. It comes from what the Queen saw of Christ in the Bible:

> *For me, the life of Jesus Christ, the Prince of Peace... is an inspiration and an anchor in my life. A role-model of reconciliation and forgiveness, he stretched out his hands in love, acceptance and healing. Christ's example has taught me to seek to respect and value all people of whatever faith or none.*

Christmas 2014

Yes, she was the Supreme Governor of the Church of England. Yes, she believed that Jesus was God, the unique Son of God, the source of forgiveness and eternal life, and strength to live this life well. Yes, she testified to his central and powerful role in her own life. She was true to herself. But part of being Christ's person was to love and honour her neighbour, whatever their beliefs.

Photo left: Listening as Holocaust camp survivors told their stories during a reception at St James's Palace on Holocaust Memorial Day, 2005

The ‘Grannie’ Who Sent Us Twister

‘She’s incredible the way she looks after everyone.’ Victoria Pryor, Goddaughter

The Queen worked hard, very hard, doing over 40 hours a week well into her nineties. It wasn’t just the engagements, it was the careful, diligent reading of the red box full of government briefings that were delivered every day. She was tremendously well informed and was, by all accounts, a significant source of thoughtful support and insightful wisdom to the 15 Prime Ministers of her reign. But she also embraced life in its fullness.

She engaged in the communities she was part of. She chose the Sunday school prizes for the children in the church at Sandringham and handed them out every year. She joined the local Women’s Institute and would pour the tea for her table just like anyone else. At Buckingham Palace she’d put on a nativity for the children of staff in the Palace stables.

Photo left: A beaming smile for the Queen’s great niece, Lady Margarita Armstrong-Jones, after attending the Christmas Day service at St Mary Magdalene’s Church, Sandringham, 2006

At Balmoral she'd go with the dogs to pick up the birds at a grouse shoot and she'd dance at the ceilidh for the gillies at the end of the season and choose appropriate books to leave in guests' bedrooms.

She was a woman who appreciated clothes that brightened a room and lifted the spirit – rich lemon, smooth lavender, soft tangerine, bright fuchsia, cool mint... She was a good sport, famously playing alongside Daniel Craig's 007 at the London Olympics, and joyously alongside Paddington Bear for her Platinum Jubilee. She loved playing silly games, driving herself, and sailing on holidays on the royal yacht, Britannia. And, of course, she loved riding. And she loved horses: breeding them, training them, racing them, and she was hugely knowledgeable about them. But they never became an obsession. Everything in its place. John Warren, the Queen's former bloodstock and racing adviser, put it this way:

Photo above: Mother and son share a joke together at the Braemar Highland Gathering in Scotland, 2017

Everyone is willing the Queen to win the Derby but Her Majesty is so wonderfully realistic. There are probably 16 runners in the race in a given year, and perhaps 15,000 horses in training. Even to have a runner in the Derby is a remarkable achievement.

I am sure it would be one of the greatest pleasures the Queen could ever have. But I know she would never sit there and ask: 'How can we win it?' Her Majesty lets fate take its course – and accepts what happens. When it comes to horses, she always looks forward and never dwells on the past. She is never melancholy. Instead, she is very level, accepting and straightforward – I suppose that is what has made her such an amazing monarch.

And of course this too stems from her understanding of Jesus, the Jesus who told his disciples to make the most of each day, who appreciated the beauty of the lilies of the field, who turned up for weddings, turned water into wine, made sure people got well fed; the Jesus who loved children and knew how to ride a never-ridden donkey through a cheering crowd throwing cloaks and palm fronds in its path; the Jesus who barbecued fish for his friends on the beach; the Jesus who came that people might have abundant life now as well as forever.

For the Queen, as for us all, the good life included doing everyday, ordinary things with joy and purpose. She had about 500 people working for her but she fed her corgis and dried their paws after walks. She'd do her own make-up and, at home, she'd often insist on making the tea. She lived in lavish surroundings, but she was modest and simple in taste. Britannia was a glorious ship but no oligarch would have been content with the relative frugality of its furnishings. She kept her cereal in Tupperware containers not porcelain jars, and if, as a young royal grandchild or great-grandchild, you might have expected a lavish Christmas present, well, you were more likely to get Twister or a set of Winnie the Pooh books. Carefully chosen but not extravagant. Indeed, some of the toys that were purchased for her own children are still being used by subsequent generations.

She wasn't a loner. She made friends and kept them. And when they died she wisely made others, from across the generations. She loved and obviously enjoyed Philip – his vigour, his advice, his humility, his sense of humour, his sharpness of mind, his curiosity about all things, his commitment to the young and the underprivileged, and

his unwavering support of her – her 'strength and stay' as she put it. And of course she had a quick sense of humour. Anecdotes abound. One day she went into a shop to pick up some groceries, and a fellow customer looked at her and said, 'You look like just like the Queen.' To which she replied, 'How very reassuring.'

Aled Jones, the BBC TV presenter, recalls meeting the Queen after singing in a concert when he was 13. At one point in his solo, he forgot the lyrics, so he made some up. The Queen congratulated him on his singing, adding, 'I rather preferred your words to the original.' Kind. And witty. Commenting on her warmth, Bishop James Newcome, who served the Queen for many years as Clerk of the Closet, said, 'Her sense of humour and her extraordinary capacity to make others feel comfortable are rooted in the serenity that comes from knowing that she's loved and called by God.'

She loved her family, remained close to her mother throughout her life, and for most of it close too to her sister.

Photo above: Prince Louis with his great grandmother on the balcony of Buckingham Palace for the Platinum Jubilee flypast, June 2022

She stuck by them all through many a difficult time, scooped up William and Harry swiftly and cared for them in Balmoral when their mother was killed. And when Andrew was embroiled in the Epstein scandal, she told him to step back from royal duties, but she took him to church the Sunday after the story broke. She was still his mother. And God the person to turn to.

As her goddaughter Victoria Pryor said,

> *She's incredible the way she looks after everyone.*

Elizabeth didn't just give us an extraordinary example of what it looks to live well as a Christian in the public eye, she gave us an inspiring example of what it looks like to live faithfully and joyfully in all of life. She made following Jesus look natural, normal, attractive, worthwhile.

Photo above: Prince William barely suppressing a grin as his grandmother inspects the troops at Sandhurst, 2006

The Queen Who Gave Us Her All

'We can surely be grateful that, 2,000 years after the birth of Jesus, so many of us are able to draw inspiration from his life and message...' Queen Elizabeth II

Elizabeth was crowned in 1952. Over 90% of us have never known anyone else on the throne.

When she was born, most Britons didn't have an inside loo, no one had a TV, and only one person had flown across the Atlantic. Today 99.9% of people have indoor loos, there are more TVs in the UK than humans, and around 5 million Brits fly to the US in an average year.

When she was born, Britain was 3% non-white, 60% of people went to church once a month or more, and there was no NHS.

Photo left: A working holiday? The Queen and her Private Secretary Sir Martin Charteris reviewing papers late at night on board HMY Britannia, 1972 (Lichfield Archive via Getty Images)

Today Britain is 16% non-white, 6% of people go to church once a month or more, and 2 million people work for the NHS.

The world has changed out of all recognition. As Elizabeth said in her Golden Jubilee speech to Parliament:

> *Change is a constant... the way we embrace it defines our future.*

And that was back in 2002, before Facebook, smartphones, and social media in general. Indeed, one of Elizabeth's great successes was her ability to change and lead change and so to keep the royal family at the heart of national life. When the public felt the monarchy was too remote from ordinary people, she changed the places they went, the people they met, and the way they related. More broadly, the wider family

Photo above: The Queen during a walkabout after unveiling a memorial to recognise the wartime sacrifices made by volunteers from the Indian subcontinent, Africa and the Caribbean, London 2002

were often ahead of the government on issues like the environment, food production and housing, whilst the younger royals worked hard to remove the taboos surrounding mental health and to support injured war veterans.

Governments have come and gone. Britain's political position in the world has declined, but admiration for the Queen has grown and grown. Despite the incessant gaze of the world's cameras, the constant scrutiny of the world's press, the thousands of people who have worked for her, there was never a whiff of scandal, or any charge of any impropriety or even bad-temperedness levelled at the Queen.

It is not just that she did the job for such a long time, it is that she did it so well for such a long time. The depth of her integrity, the quality of her kindness and the strength of her commitment to

Photo above: Children from Crathie Primary School presenting a card after the Queen and Prince Charles planted a tree as part of the Queen's Green Canopy, Balmoral, Scotland, 2021

serving her country's best interests, to valuing each person, and to summoning us to give of our best have all served to increase the love, affection, and respect that people feel for her. 'Amazing' is the word that many use.

She has been like a beacon on a hill, steady and bright, all of most of our lives. And for her shining, selfless example and extraordinary contribution to nation and Commonwealth we owe her a huge debt of gratitude.

Elizabeth, ever modest, would of course not want the last words to be about her. She would point to Jesus as her inspiration, the source of her success and of her happiness:

> *He (Jesus) makes it clear that genuine human happiness and satisfaction lie more in giving than receiving; more in serving than in being served. We can surely be grateful that, two thousand years after the birth of Jesus, so many of us are able to draw inspiration from his life and message, and to find in him a source of strength and courage.*

Surely we have reason to share the Queen's gratitude for the inspiration and strength she drew from him. After all, have we not seen the prayers of our national anthem answered by the God Elizabeth served and loved?

For our Queen was gracious.

She was noble.

She was happy and glorious.

God did send her.

She did reign long over us and she faithfully fulfilled her calling.

And God saved her.

As he is willing to save all of us.

Thanks be to him for the gift of Elizabeth, his, and our, servant Queen.

Photo right: Arriving for the State Opening of Parliament in London, 2013

Working in over 240 countries and territories, Bible Society is on a mission to offer the Bible to everyone, in England, Wales and around the world. This is because we believe that when people engage with the Scriptures lives can be changed, for good.

Find out more about Bible Society's work at **biblesociety.org.uk**

The Queen's life of faith and service, and her testimony to Jesus, was an inspiration. HOPE Together longs to see everyone everywhere knowing Jesus. HOPE encourages, equips, resources and inspires Christians and local churches to work together to share the good news of Jesus through what we say and what we do.

Find out more about HOPE's work at **hopetogether.org.uk**

LICC exists to empower Christians to make a difference with Jesus in daily life. Her Majesty Queen Elizabeth II was an exemplary whole-life disciple of Jesus, integrating her faith into everything she did. Through resources, training, events, videos, and more, LICC helps Christians across the UK do the same - for the glory of God and the life of the world.

Find out more about LICC's work at **licc.org.uk**

Photography Credits
All photos are from Alamy apart from:
Front Cover – Jane Bown / Camera Press
p.2 – Anwar Hussein / Getty Images
p.27 – Ron Bell / Camera Press
p.41 – Anwar Hussein / Getty Images
p.58 – Lichfield Archive via Getty Images

Author
Mark Greene, LICC

Editor
Catherine Butcher, HOPE Together

Designer
Claire Simmons-Clark, Bible Society

With special thanks to Roy Crowne, Paul Woolley, Stuart Noble